THE NATIONAL TRUST

Investigating TRANSPORT

By Julie Smart
Illustrated by Edward Ripley
Cover illustration by Merida Woodford

Contents

Paving the way	2
Back to the tracks	4
Travel in style	6
All at sea	8
Ship shape	10
The canal age	12
Railway mania	14
On the right lines	16
From boneshakers to BMX	18
Horseless carriages	20
Big business	22
Transport takes off!	24
Tickets to ride	26
Safe journey!	28
Shades of green	30
Note to parents/Answers	32

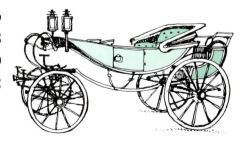

Paving the way

They came, they saw, they built roads...

The Romans are famous for their roads. It's hardly surprising when you think that some of them are still used today – more than 1,500 years after they were built.

Before the Romans came to Britain in AD43 the only means of travel between settlements or villages was on foot or horseback (if you were rich enough to own a horse) along narrow, winding tracks, footpaths and ridge ways.

Good roads were required to control a large empire. The Romans had to move troops and supplies quickly, they wanted to trade in valuable resources, and they also needed links between their growing number of towns or settlements.

The straight and narrow

Every Roman legion had its own skilled road engineer. They made sure that the roads were built following the shortest – and therefore straightest – route between two places.

They were made just wide enough for two companies of soldiers – or two wagons – to pass each other. Layers of stones were covered with gravel and then topped with slabs of smooth stone. The roads had a camber or curved surface so water would run off into drainage ditches dug on either side. Milestones placed along roads at distances of 1,000 Roman paces (1,480 metres) told people how far they had to go before reaching the next town. (The Latin word for one thousand was 'mille'.)

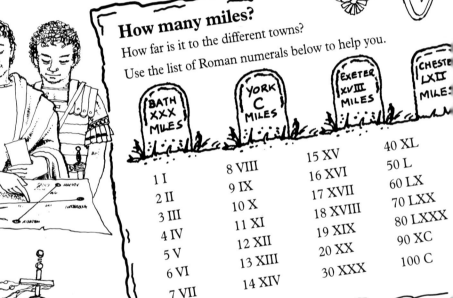

How many miles?

How far is it to the different towns? Use the list of Roman numerals below to help you.

BATH XXX MILES
YORK C MILES
EXETER XVIII MILES
CHESTER LXII MILES

1 I	8 VIII	15 XV	40 XL
2 II	9 IX	16 XVI	50 L
3 III	10 X	17 XVII	60 LX
4 IV	11 XI	18 XVIII	70 LXX
5 V	12 XII	19 XIX	80 LXXX
6 VI	13 XIII	20 XX	90 XC
7 VII	14 XIV	30 XXX	100 C

On the march

Imagine walking from London to Newcastle! That's what Roman soldiers would have had to do to join the legions building Hadrian's Wall on the northernmost border of the Roman Empire. They could march an average of about 20 miles a day. How long would it have taken them if it is 300 miles? (Answer on page 32.) Today it takes about 7 hours by car, 3 hours by train and only 1 hour 10 minutes by plane!

Coast to coast

When Emperor Hadrian visited Britain in AD 122 he ordered the building of a huge wall, stretching from Newcastle on the east coast to Carlisle in the west, to keep out the northern tribes or barbarians and mark the northern-most limit of the Roman Empire.

The wall was a great engineering feat, standing about 5 metres high and 3 metres thick. Small forts at intervals of one Roman mile were built along its length, linked by a road called Stanegate.

The National Trust owns a stretch of the wall from Housesteads to Steel Rigg, including Housesteads Fort. You can walk along the wall and imagine what it must have been like to be a Roman soldier. In the museum, plans and models show you what the fort would have looked like when it was first built.

Life of luxury

One of the main Roman roads in Britain was the Fosse Way, a major trade route which linked Exeter and Lincoln. Near to this road, at Chedworth in Gloucestershire, are the remains of a Roman villa which can still be visited. Big farming estates often had a central group of buildings, called a villa, and this one was particularly luxurious. It had two elaborate bath complexes and under floor heating. There are a number of villa sites in this area, whose prosperity was probably due to easy access to the thriving market towns of Cirencester and Gloucester provided by the nearby Fosse Way.

Did you know…

That you can still walk along some stretches of Roman road? The best preserved section of Roman road in Britain runs across the moors at Blackstone Edge on the border between Lancashire and Yorkshire.

If you're in the area, perhaps walking at Hardcastle Crags, near Hebden Bridge, or visiting East Riddlesden Hall near Keighley, it's well worth a visit. There's another stretch at Blackpool Bridge near Blakeney in Gloucestershire.

Clues to the past

Roman roads can be spotted on maps quite easily because they are so straight. Have a look at a modern road map and see if you can see any. They often link towns that were important settlements in Roman times - look for names of towns ending in -caster, -cester or -chester from the Roman word casta meaning a camp. (Chester, Cirencester, Gloucester, Leicester, Winchester, Dorchester.)

Here are some of the most famous roads:

Watling Street (Dover - Chester)

Fosse Way (Exeter - Lincoln)

Ermine Street (London - Lincoln - York)

Akeman Street (London - Bath)

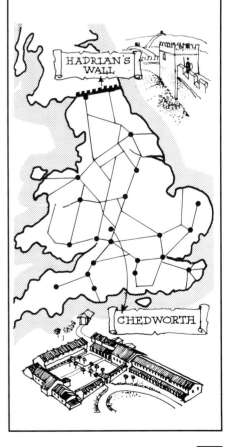

Back to the tracks

The road to ruin

When the Romans left Britain in AD 410, people carried on using their roads, but since they didn't know how to maintain them and, furthermore, couldn't see why they needed to, the roads quickly fell into disrepair. So everyone went back to using the old winding tracks, searching for fords to cross streams or using packhorse or stone 'clapper' bridges. These were bridges made of stone slabs or wooden planks resting on piles of stones.

Many of our country roads follow the same routes as early farmers or traders with their wagons and carts. Some farmers would herd their animals for miles along tracks such as the famous cattle drovers' route from Wales to the Midlands which runs along a ridge in Shropshire called The Long Mynd.

Nowhere to go?

In an age when most families have a car, do we take transport for granted? We catch buses to work and school, we go shopping by car and on holiday by train or even plane. Our whole way of life today means that we have come to rely on being able to travel easily to different places. So how did people manage before the invention of the car? The train? The aeroplane? Before there were even proper roads?

Our reasons for travel are very different from early times. In the past, most people lived in self-sufficient communities and didn't need to travel great distances. They grew their own food, made their own clothes and built their homes from local materials. There was no reason for them to leave their town or village. That's why Roman roads were allowed to deteriorate.

It could be fun to carry out a survey. How many different forms of transport do you use in one day, one week, one year? Ask your friends or parents. What about your grandparents? How much have things changed since they were children? You could make a chart like the one opposite.

Name: _____	Bike	Car	Train	Bus	Plane	Boat	Horse	Foot
Monday								
Tuesday								
Wednesday								
Thusrsday								
Friday								
Saturday								
Sunday								

Highways and by-ways

Roads regained their importance during the Middle Ages. Landowners or lords would visit their manors and estates by horse, litter or wagon. Traders and merchants relied on packhorses. Their well-worn tracks became known as the public 'highway'.

The Church helped to maintain the roads – good roads made it easier to manage the many farms run by monasteries and also meant that people could get to church more easily!

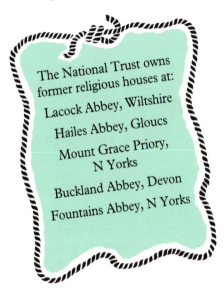

The National Trust owns former religious houses at:

Lacock Abbey, Wiltshire

Hailes Abbey, Gloucs

Mount Grace Priory, N Yorks

Buckland Abbey, Devon

Fountains Abbey, N Yorks

Then, in 1534, Henry VIII made himself head of the Church of England and began to close down all the religious houses to reduce the power of the Church and to sell them at a profit. This meant that monks and nuns could no longer help with the upkeep of roads. So a special law was passed in 1555 requiring two people each year from every parish to decide what repairs needed to be made. All householders were then supposed to help out with the work.

What would you think if you had to go out and mend the road outside your house? Exactly! No-one did it then either! So a fine was introduced for those who refused to do the work.

Pay up or else…!

Things went from bad to worse – roads were really nothing more than dirt tracks which became so muddy in bad weather they couldn't be used.

Something had to be done.

The Turnpike Act 1663 was a law which made the people who used the roads pay for their upkeep. Spiked wooden barriers, or turnpikes, were placed across the road at various points. Once you had paid the fee or toll to the toll-keeper he would raise the barrier. The money went to the people who looked after the roads.

But some people wouldn't pay and a further Act was passed in 1728 which said that anyone found guilty of breaking down a tollgate would be sentenced to three months in jail and a public whipping! The Act made no difference and in 1735 it was changed to the death penalty.

Clues to the past

There are still some toll-keeper's cottages standing today. Is there one near you? We sometimes pay tolls in this country to cross bridges and on the Continent we pay to use motor ways.

Travel in style

On the wagon

Horse-drawn vehicles in the Middle Ages were little more than tents on wheels! The only protection from the wind and rain was a cover called an awning. Later, they were made more comfortable – they had proper roofs, glass windows instead of leather curtains and the chassis (or frame) was suspended between the wheels to make the ride less bumpy. These were the first real coaches and soon the fashion for better private coaches and open carriages led to the design of models such as the brougham, landau and phaeton.

Horse-drawn coaches offering a passenger service first appeared in the early 1600s. They were known as stage wagons because they stopped at 'stages' of about ten miles, usually inns, where fresh horses were kept for hire to the coach companies and where passengers could rest and have something to eat.

Mail coaches which provided a postal service between London and other large cities were soon reaching speeds of nearly 12mph (or 20 km/hr) – and that was considered fast!

Brougham

Barouche

Landau

Clues to the past

If your surname is WHEELER, CARTWRIGHT, SMITH or CARTER, your ancestors may have had connections with horse transport. In the Middle Ages, when people first began using surnames, some people adopted their family's trade or occupation to distinguish them from others with the same Christian name. Hence:

WHEELER – maker of wheels (also WRIGHT from WHEELWRIGHT)

CARTWRIGHT – maker of carts

SMITH – worker in metal, possibly blacksmith or shoesmith

CARTER – a waggoner, transporter of goods or stable headman

SUMPTER – driver of a packhorse (also SUNTER, SUMMER)

Collectors items

Carts and carriages of every shape and size are on display at Arlington Court in Devon. From Queen Victoria's pony bath chair to a dog cart designed to be pulled by a St Bernard, the collection gives some idea of the vehicles which might have been found in a typical nineteenth-century country house. There are landaus and broughams, phaetons and wagonettes, gigs and buggies – there are even children's carriages and perambulators (prams)!

There are also carriage collections at:

Calke Abbey, Derbyshire

Erdigg, Clwyd

The Argory, Co Armagh, Northern Ireland

There are carts in the thatched barn at Wimpole Farm, Cambridgeshire

Many National Trust houses have stable blocks. One of the oldest is at Dunster Castle in Somerset, which was probably built in the 1600s. There are others at Saltram, Dunham Massey and Charlecote.

All change

A famous coaching terminus – rather like an eighteenth-century bus station – still stands in London. In the eighteenth and nineteenth centuries, coaches left The George Inn in Southwark for destinations throughout England. It was even mentioned by Dickens in 'Little Dorrit'. The George is now the last galleried inn left in London, though you can no longer stay there overnight.

Another old coaching inn is the King's Head in Aylesbury, which still has its old cobbled stable yard.

Lacock village in Wiltshire was a staging post on the road linking centres of the wool trade in the west country. A narrow lane leads from the church to the eighteenth-century packhorse bridge over the Bide Brook and beyond to the Avon.

Early traffic polution

There may have been no pollution from car exhaust fumes but imagine what streets would have been like full of horse dung and flies! People then didn't understand the importance of cleanliness and sanitation to prevent the spread of disease.

Great road builders

In the late 1700s, thanks to the skills of three men, Britain once again had roads that people could use – whatever the weather.

John (Blind Jack) Metcalf (1717-1810) realised that sharper stones made better road surfaces than round stones which were easily dislodged by horses' hooves and wheels. To Thomas Telford (1757-1834) we owe the London to Holyhead Road (still in use as the A5) plus a whole network of Scottish roads and canals. John McAdam (1756-1836) used crushed and broken stones to make a compact road. In 1882, the method was improved by covering the stones with tar – hence the name tarmacadam, now shortened to tarmac.

Stand and deliver

Roads were dangerous places in the eighteenth century, just as they are today. Coaches could overturn in the mud or on dry ruts and highwaymen were always a threat to travellers. Coachmen carried a type of gun called a blunderbuss for security. Many highwaymen worked in league with innkeepers, who knew the times when coaches would be running and could get inside information on the passengers – in other words, find out if they were likely to be carrying valuables.

The most notorious highwayman was Dick Turpin, who became almost a living legend because of his escapades. One famous tale – and it is only a tale – is that he galloped on his horse, Black Bess, from Essex to York in record time to establish an alibi. But the law eventually caught up with him and on 10 April 1739, he was hanged in York for murder.

Clues to the past

Old forges – or cottages perhaps now called 'The Old Forge' – are reminders of the times when horses were the main means of transport and farriers were needed to replace worn horse-shoes. Other evidence to look out for includes local inn signs ('The Coach and Horses'), mounting blocks and horse troughs.

All at sea

A seafaring nation

Britain is an island and so it is only natural that ships should have played an important part in its history. For many hundred of years, ships were the best means of communication between people in different parts of the world. Not only did they carry cargoes of goods for trade but they also provided the means to invade and settle in other countries, from the early Roman and Viking invasions of Britain to the first colonists of the 'New World' of America and later Australia.

Some of this country's greatest heroes have been seafarers.

Sir Francis Drake is famous for being the first Englishman to sail around the world. He was also an important commander of the English fleet which fought against the Spanish Armada in 1588. Drake, so the story goes, was playing bowls when he heard news of the Armada's arrival and he is supposed to have said 'We have time to finish the game and beat the Spaniards'!

Beware the beating drum!

Buckland Abbey in Devon was the home of Sir Francis Drake.

He bought the house in 1581, after completing his journey round the world and it was from here that he planned his assault on the Spanish Armada a few years later.

Some fascinating relics are on display. There are flags which may have flown on his ship, the 'Golden Hind' when he made his epic voyage; Armada medals, the first to commemorate a historical event; and finds from Spanish ships that foundered off Ireland and Scotland, as well as documents and accounts about the Armada.

But perhaps most interesting of all is Drake's Drum which, legend has it, will start to beat if England is ever in danger.

After a number of battles at sea, in which ships from both sides were badly damaged, some of the ships from the fleeing Armada tried to get back to Spain by sailing round Ireland's and Scotland's treacherous coasts. Many were wrecked. You can see the spot where the ship 'Girona' sank on the rocks at Port na Spaniagh, near The Giant's Causeway, County Antrim.

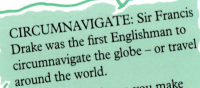

CIRCUMNAVIGATE: Sir Francis Drake was the first Englishman to circumnavigate the globe – or travel around the world.

How many words can you make from the word 'circumnavigate'? There are at least 50. (See page 32.)

Who goes there?

Draw a line to match the sailor to their achievement. (Answers on page 32.)

Christopher Columbus   - made the first voyage round the world

Vasco da Gama   - was the first Englishman to sail round the world

Ferdinand Magellan   - discovered the Americas for Spain

Sir Francis Drake   - discovered a sea route from Europe to India

The age of discovery

Christopher Columbus (c. 1451 – 1506) believed that the world was round not flat, unlike people in the Middle Ages. He said that if you were to sail west you would eventually reach the East and China and Japan, which were thought to be places of great riches. What he did not know was that the Americas and the West Indies lay in the way of this westward route to the east. Columbus was actually Italian, although his first language was Spanish, and Queen Isabella of Spain sponsored his journeys.

On 2 August 1492, Columbus and his crew set sail from Spain and headed west across the Atlantic. On 12 October they landed on an island near America we now call San Salvador. He didn't actually reach the mainland of South America until his third voyage in 1498.

Sir Humphrey Gilbert was another intrepid explorer who in June 1583 set sail across the Atlantic from Plymouth in his frigate 'The Squirrel' and discovered Newfoundland. Tragically, on his return voyage his ship sank and he drowned. Hundreds of years later Sir Humphrey's descendants settled at Trelissick, near Truro, Cornwall. The estate water tower there is crowned with a squirrel weather-vane in his memory.

Sir Walter Raleigh, Sir Humphrey Gilbert's half-brother, sailed to South America in 1595 in search of an imaginary land of gold called El Dorado – which he never found.

By the time he returned, James I had succeeded Elizabeth on the throne. James was suspicious of Raleigh and locked him in the Tower of London for 12 years. On his release, Raleigh went back to South America, but when he returned again without gold and treasure, King James had him executed.

Clues to the past

How many things can you find in your kitchen cupboards that we have the great explorers to thank for? Early travellers brought back commodities we now take for granted such as salt, sugar, tea and coffee as well as spices. Don't forget the common potato, which would have been considered quite exotic when it was brought back from North America in the late 1500s – not by Sir Walter Raleigh, as most people believe, but by two captains whom Raleigh had sent across the Atlantic to claim land for Elizabeth I.

Ship shape

Transatlantic trips

In 1818, the American ship 'Savannah' crossed the Atlantic under combined sail and steam power. In 1837, the 'Sirius' made the same crossing under steam power alone, arriving in New York from Cork having burned all the coal on board plus the wooden cabin furniture, and a mast! It was followed only a few hours later by the purpose-built Atlantic steamer 'Great Western', designed by Isambard Kingdom Brunel, which docked with 200 tons of coal left in the bunkers after its longer voyage from Bristol.

Brunel's next masterpiece was the 'Great Eastern', the largest ship ever built at that time. This too was a paddle steamer with sails but it was made of iron and had propellers. There were 4,000 passengers aboard on its first Atlantic crossing in 1860.

Did you know that...

The National Trust cares for boats as well as houses?

An elegant Victorian steam yacht, restored by the Trust, still takes passengers on trips around Coniston Water in the Lake District. The 'Gondola' was originally launched as a tourist attraction in 1860 by the Furness Railway Company after they had completed their rail link to Coniston Water.

Supremacy on the seas

Trafalgar Square in London is a monument to an important battle that confirmed Britian's supremacy on the world's seas. Admiral Horatio Nelson, in 'HMS Victory', led the British fleet to victory against the French and Spanish at the Battle of Trafalgar on 21 October 1805.

It was King Henry VIII who established the first real British navy. His battleship best known to us was 'Mary Rose', which sank in the Solent on its maiden voyage in 1545. Modern technology has enabled the wreck to be raised from the sea bed and it is on view in the Royal Naval Museum in Portsmouth.

A life on the ocean wave!

In 1840, a Canadian called Samuel Cunard began a regular mail service between Britain and North America with his paddle steamer 'Britannia'. This ship made the Atlantic crossing from Liverpool to Halifax, Nova Scotia, and on to Boston, in 14 days.

In 1907, the Cunard company launched the 'Mauretania', which won the coveted 'Blue Riband' award for the fastest crossing. Soon, big shipping companies were competing against each other to build the biggest, fastest, most luxurious liners for the North Atlantic route.

Perhaps the two greatest rivals were the French built 'Normandie' and Cunard's 'Queen Mary'. The 'Normandie' even had indoor swimming pools, a cinema and dance hall.

By the 1950s, the average crossing was made in well under four days. Nowadays, jet aircraft take only a matter of hours and the few liners left, such as the 'Queen Elizabeth II (QE2)', take passengers on luxury cruises.

SOS

There have been a number of famous maritime disasters or shipwrecks.

The 'Titanic' was supposedly built so that it would never sink, but on the night of 14 April 1912, 1,522 men, women and children lost their lives when one of the biggest and most luxurious passenger liners ever launched hit an iceberg in the North Atlantic on her maiden voyage.

The 'Lusitania' was a British passenger ship that sank near Ireland after being torpedoed by a German submarine during the First World War; 1,198 people died. The German government claimed it was a legal target because it was armed and carrying war materials.

The 'Bismarck' was a German battleship sunk by the British during the Second World War. It was one of the most powerful battleships afloat.

Other National Trust properties with seafaring links include:

COMPTON CASTLE, Devon, home of the Gilbert family, which in the sixteenth century had three brothers who all became famous for their seafaring actions: John was a vice-admiral and helped defeat the Spanish Armada; his younger brothers, Humphrey and Adrian, were explorers. Their half-brother was Walter Raleigh.

OVERBECKS MUSEUM, Devon, is an Edwardian house overlooking the sea and the former home of scientist Otto Overbeck. On display there is everything from sailors' snuffboxes to marine paintings and model ships.

There are more model ships to be seen at ARLINGTON COURT, Devon, mostly collected by Rosalie Chichester on her many travels, including one of Sir Francis Chichester's famous yacht, 'Gipsy Moth IV'. Sir Francis was Rosalie's step-nephew.

In the grounds of SHUGBOROUGH, Staffordshire, there is a monument dedicated to a cat which travelled with his master on a four-year voyage round the world! George Anson made his circumnavigation of the globe in the 1740s during which he captured a treasure laden Spanish galleon. Much of the Admiral's wealth went to help his elder brother Thomas improve Shugborough Hall, which has been the home of the Anson family since 1624.

MELFORD HALL in Suffolk was bought by the seafaring Parker family in 1786. Three members of the family were admirals and the pictures in the library show some of their experiences at sea.

Did you know that...

Sir Francis Chichester set the record for sailing single-handed across the Atlantic. In 1966-7, he sailed round the world in his yacht, 'Gipsy Moth IV', in 226 days. He was knighted with a sword that once belonged to Sir Francis Drake.

In 1976, Clare Francis was the only woman to finish the Royal Western Single-handed Transatlantic Race. She set a women's record of 29 days in her yacht 'Robertson's Golly'.

The canal age

Coal, cotton and cattle

Today you can walk along towpaths, go fishing on canal banks or enjoy a trip on a passenger boat, but canals were really built as industrial waterways.

Rivers had always been used for transport but with the growth of industry in the eighteenth century in places not easily reached by navigated rivers, the new factories needed a quick and cheap means of getting coal and other raw materials as well as of distributing the goods they made. Horse-drawn vehicles were simply not suitable.

The first canal opened in 1761, linking a coal mine in Worsley owned by the Duke of Bridgewater, with Manchester. The Bridgewater Canal was heralded as a great success. Soon, hundreds of miles of canal linked Britain's new factories and fast-growing towns and cities.

Almost anything could be carried by water – from cotton to cattle, iron, manure, bricks, corn, salt and always coal.

Back to barges?

Just think what a difference it would make if we went back to using barges for carrying cargo – no heavy lorries on our roads, less traffic jams and less pollution. Some European countries are enlarging their canals and even digging new ones. Should we be doing the same?

Leg work

The first boats were horse drawn – it was only later that they were powered by steam and then diesel. One horse could pull or tow a boat – that's why the path beside the canal, along which the horse walked, is called a towpath. When they reached a tunnel, the boatmen had to 'leg' boats through, lying down and walking their feet on the walls or roof, while the horses walked over the top.

The RIVER WEY AND GODALMING NAVIGATIONS, built in 1670, is one of the earliest historic waterways and is a navigable river, not a specially dug canal. A 20-mile stretch between Godalming Wharf and the Thames at Weybridge in Surrey is owned by the Trust. In its heyday, the Navigations would have been busy with traffic carrying timber and agricultural produce down to London, while corn and general merchandise was brought up to Guildford and Godalming. It is still a busy stretch of water, but these days the boats are pleasure craft. At Dapdune Wharf in Guildford you can see a restored horse-drawn barge.

The ROYAL MILITARY CANAL in Kent was never intended for transport. It was dug to keep out Napoleon and his army should they ever try to invade England. However, once the threat of a French invasion was over, it was made suitable for commercial traffic.

You can travel by barge down the Bridgewater Canal from Manchester to DUNHAM MASSEY in Cheshire.

Wilbraham Egerton, first Earl of Tatton (TATTON PARK, Cheshire), was chairman of the board of the Manchester Ship Canal Company between 1832 and 1909.

When RUFFORD OLD HALL in Lancashire was altered by Sir Thomas Hesketh in the 1820s, most of the building materials were transported by canal – in fact, the Leeds and Liverpool Canal runs so close to the hall that several estate buildings had to be demolished when it was built!

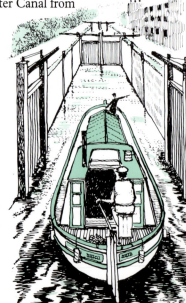

Up hills and across valleys

Water cannot flow up hills – at least not without help! Engineers such as James Brindley (1716-1772) and Thomas Telford (1757-1834) overcame this problem in several ways. Where the hills were not too steep they built locks. By opening and closing the gates the locks raised or lowered the barges from one water level to another. With steeper hills, a staircase of locks was sometimes needed, such as the one at Foxton, near Market Harborough in Leicestershire.

Aqueducts were built to carry canals across valleys. James Brindley built the first one at Barton near Manchester, to take the Bridgewater Canal across the River Irwell. When he first announced his plans, people thought he was mad – but it worked!

Roses and castles

The brightly painted narrow boats, built for the narrow locks of the Midlands canals, are well known for the traditional 'roses and castles' design which appears on the side alongside the name of the boat and its owner. Each canal company had its own colours and style of lettering but the pictures were always basically the same – roses, a castle, a bridge, sailing boats and mountains in the background. Even the cans for drinking water which stand on the cabin roof are decorated.

Did you know that...

You can go from London to York and from Norfolk to Wales by inland waterway?

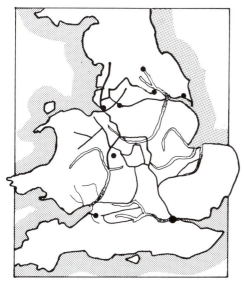

The coming of railways

In 1830, the Liverpool and Manchester Railway opened in direct competition with the Bridgewater Canal. It was faster and cheaper – the canal companies couldn't compete. Some railway companies even bought up canals to stop them being used. The invention of the motor car at the turn of the century finally sealed the fate of Britain's canals.

The Inland Waterways Association campaigns to stop canals being closed and organises voluntary restoration work. Many derelict canals have now been re-opened for people to enjoy and the canal environment is a haven for many species of wildlife.

Clues to the past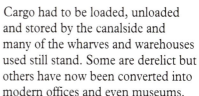

Cargo had to be loaded, unloaded and stored by the canalside and many of the wharves and warehouses used still stand. Some are derelict but others have now been converted into modern offices and even museums.

Look out, too, for old lock-keepers' cottages, many now privately owned.

Do you know of any local canalside pubs, which would once have enjoyed a thriving trade from passing thirsty boatmen? Popular pub names include 'The Navigation', 'The Boat', and 'The Wharf'.

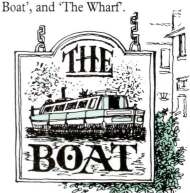

Railway mania

Iron Roads

Railways existed long before steam engines were invented.

Mines had wooden tracks along which to roll wagons full of coal – and it was men who had to do the rolling! Iron eventually replaced wood and wagon wheels were given flanges to keep them on the rails. Horses could now safely pull much heavier loads.

The father of the railways

George Stephenson was born in 1781 in a small one-roomed cottage beside the River Tyne near Wylam in Northumberland. The only way to get there is still by foot or bicycle. In front of the house is the track of the old Wylam Colliery wagon way, now a riverside walk, for which Richard Trevithick had produced an early steam engine.

Full steam ahead!

The world's first steam locomotive was built by a Cornish engineer, Richard Trevithick. In 1808, the 'Catch Me Who Can' pulled a four-wheeled carriage round a circular track near what is now Euston Station in London.

Trevithick's earlier inventions included a high pressure steam engine which could pump hundreds of litres of water a minute out of the Cornish tin mines to stop them flooding. These amazing engines also took miners and ore up and down the mine shafts. If you want to see a working engine, contact the manager at South Crofty Mine, which is owned by the National Trust. Richard Trevithick's whitewashed thatched cottage at Lower Penponds, Camborne, is also a Trust property.

Others soon followed Trevithick's lead and five years later, in 1813, 'Puffing Billy' was built by William Hedley for the Wylam Colliery Railway near Newcastle-upon-Tyne. It was used to haul coal wagons from the colliery to the nearby River Tyne, a job previously done by horses.

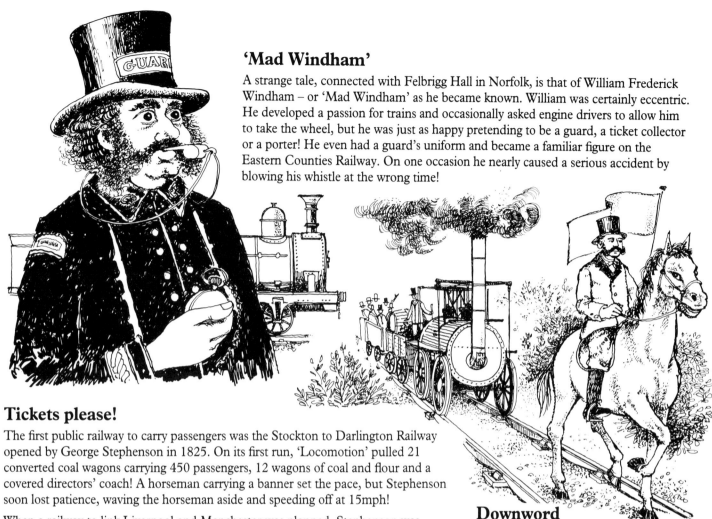

'Mad Windham'

A strange tale, connected with Felbrigg Hall in Norfolk, is that of William Frederick Windham – or 'Mad Windham' as he became known. William was certainly eccentric. He developed a passion for trains and occasionally asked engine drivers to allow him to take the wheel, but he was just as happy pretending to be a guard, a ticket collector or a porter! He even had a guard's uniform and became a familiar figure on the Eastern Counties Railway. On one occasion he nearly caused a serious accident by blowing his whistle at the wrong time!

Tickets please!

The first public railway to carry passengers was the Stockton to Darlington Railway opened by George Stephenson in 1825. On its first run, 'Locomotion' pulled 21 converted coal wagons carrying 450 passengers, 12 wagons of coal and flour and a covered directors' coach! A horseman carrying a banner set the pace, but Stephenson soon lost patience, waving the horseman aside and speeding off at 15mph!

When a railway to link Liverpool and Manchester was planned, Stephenson was appointed chief engineer. In 1829, a competition was held to find a fast and reliable locomotive for the new line. At the Rainhill trials, George Stephenson's 'Rocket' amazed the world by reaching a speed of just over 30mph (48km/hr). No vehicle – or person for that matter! – had ever travelled so fast before and doctors warned that at such speeds people would be unable to breathe and even ran the risk of their lungs bursting!

Out of the four steam locos which entered the trials, 'Rocket' was the only one to finish. The Liverpool and Manchester Railway opened in 1830 with six trains running daily. 'Railway Mania' had well and truly begun. George Stephenson (1781-1848) and his son, Robert (1803-1859), along with Isambard Kingdom Brunel, constructed huge iron bridges and stone viaducts to carry tracks across rivers and valleys. Brunel (1806-1859) was responsible for designing many of the great railways, bridges and tunnels in Britain.

By 1850 there were more than 7,000 miles (11,000 km) of track throughout the British Isles and railways could offer passengers luxurious facilities such as heating, lighting and toilets!

Downword

Fill in the names of the main London railway stations to complete this downword. We have given you the first letters to help you. What word can you read across? (Answer on page 32.)

On the right lines

Battle of the gauges

Things happened so quickly that railways sprang up here and there all over the country. Rival companies competed over the best land and routes, their 'navvies' working hard to dig cuttings and embankments. (Their name actually came from the word 'navigator', applied to the workers who had dug the canal network.) The tracks they laid were mainly to Stephenson's 'standard' gauge, or width, of 4 feet 8½ inches.

Then came Brunel and the Great Western Railway, which ran between London and Bristol. Brunel decided that by making the tracks 7ft wide, he could use more powerful locomotives and bigger carriages. It took a Parliamentary Commission to settle the matter in an attempt to end the confusion. In 1846, it was decided that 4 feet 8.5 inches ('narrow gauge') would be the norm and the Great Western was gradually converted to a three-rail 'mixed gauge'.

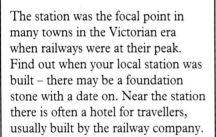

Clues to the past

The station was the focal point in many towns in the Victorian era when railways were at their peak. Find out when your local station was built – there may be a foundation stone with a date on. Near the station there is often a hotel for travellers, usually built by the railway company.

People started up businesses along the track, making it easier for them to transport their goods. Look at a map of your nearest large town. Are there buildings near the railway lines? They could be factories, workshops, breweries or warehouses. Are they still there today?

There may be rows of terraced houses built from bricks and slates which are not local materials. They would have been brought by rail from another part of the country.

From steam to electric

Railways had a tremendous impact on all aspects of life. People could travel from place to place in a fraction of the time it had previously taken by coach, and many more people could now afford to travel. People living in the country could commute to work in nearby cities. City dwellers could go on trips to the country or seaside. Huge loads of coal, timber and manufactured goods could be transported in as many hours as it had previously taken days or even weeks by road, barge or sailing ship.

But the railway had its opponents, too. They complained about the possible effects on health – the noise, the smell of oil and smoke, not to mention the soot and grime polluting the air.

Rail travel remained the most important means of transport right up till the mid 1900s. The fastest and largest steam locomotives ever built ran in the 1930s and '40s. In 1938 the British locomotive 'Mallard' achieved a record 203 km/hr. But steam eventually gave way to diesel and electric.

The first electric trains were developed towards the end of the nineteenth century. Some locos collected power from overhead cables, others from a third live rail on the track. Electricity is faster, quieter and cleaner, and although it is expensive to build the lines in the first place, electric trains are economic to run.

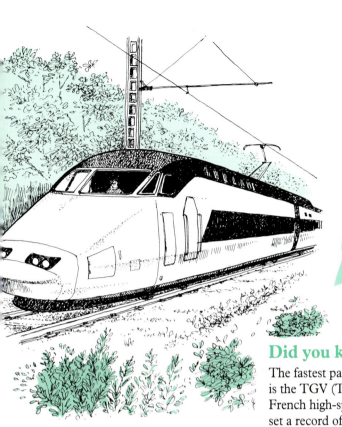

At SALTRAM in Devon there is an old steam railway engine on display.

Visit CORFE CASTLE in Dorset by steam train! The old branch line from Dorchester to Corfe Castle has now been re-opened by the Swanage Steam Railway.

A special train line was built by the owner of CASTLE DROGO in Devon to transport granite from the quarry to the building site when the house was being built.

Deep underground beneath MARSDEN MOOR, West Yorkshire, lies the eight-mile long Standedge Tunnel on the railway from Ashton under Lyne to Huddersfield. This was one of the great engineering feats of the nineteenth century.

Don't miss the railway museum at PENRHYN CASTLE, Gwynedd, where there are locomotives and trucks once used in the slate quarries as well as a model railway.

Did you know that…

The fastest passenger train in the world is the TGV (Train à Grande Vitesse), a French high-speed electric train, which set a record of 515 km/hr in 1990.

Trains and boats and planes… What am I?

The names below belong to a famous train, ship or aeroplane. Do you know which? Write the names in the correct shapes.

Great Eastern	Voyager	Rocket
Mary Rose	Concorde	Catch Me Who Can
Titanic	Jason	Puffing Billy
Golden Hind	Spirit of St Louis	Mallard

(Turn to page 32 for the answers.)

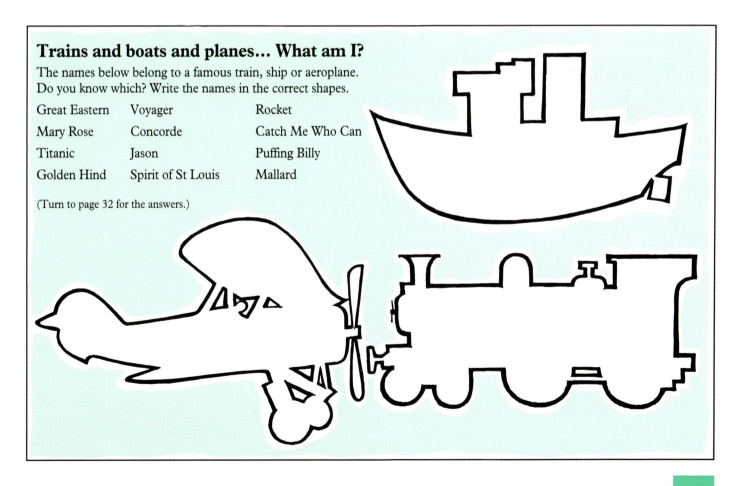

From boneshakers to BMX

Meals on wheels?

Riding bicycles is fun, but don't forget that it is also a means of transport. There was a time when they were one of the fastest vehicles on the road and many goods, especially food, were delivered by errand boys on bicycles. Do you know anyone today who uses a bicycle to help them with their job? What about your postman or woman? For really fast deliveries some people now use motorbike couriers and motorcycles play an important part for traffic police.

Pedal power

The very first bicycle was designed by a German, Baron von Drais, in the early 1800s. It had two wheels connected by a wooden beam, a saddle and handlebars – but no pedals! It was more like a walking machine because the way to move was to push yourself along with your feet! In fact, it was called a 'velocipede', meaning a vehicle propelled by the feet, although it was better known as the hobby-horse.

Later, pedals and a crank were fixed to the front wheel hub. One turn of the pedals meant one turn of the wheel. These 'boneshakers' with wooden wheels were very uncomfortable – hence the name! To go faster, designers made the front wheel larger. The result was the penny farthing, so called because its big and little wheels reminded people of the two coins – the penny and the farthing (the farthing was worth a quarter of an old penny). Its proper name is an ordinary. The front wheel eventually became so big that it was too difficult even to get on – and a long way down to fall!

Eventually, the front wheel was made smaller again so that the rider could reach the floor and the pedals were placed between the wheels. Gears meant that they still went as fast as the ordinaries and the addition of steering made the machines even safer – they were called safety cycles! The invention of the air-filled pneumatic tyre in 1888 by J B Dunlop, who was British, made bicycles more comfortable and easier to ride.

In the hot seat

In the 1860s the French firm Michaux built the original boneshaker. In 1869 they fitted a tiny steam engine to one of their bikes. It was not very successful – the driver's seat was above the boiler!

In 1885, Gottlieb Daimler, a German who is more famous for inventing the motor car, tried his petrol engine for the first time in a wooden bike, but it was Hildebrand and Wolfmuller of Germany who around 1894 made the Motorrad, the first true motorbike. It had a small twin cylinder engine and could travel at 28 mph (45 km/h), which was faster than most cars of the time. Britain built up a thriving motorcycle industry led by companies such as Leyland. It is only recently that competition from Japan has contributed to its decline.

Did you know that

The first Honda machines were reconditioned army vehicles from the Second World War. Soichiro Honda, who founded the company that bears his name, went on to build the biggest motorcycle business ever known.

Safe cycling!

Today, most children own a bike. There are even special tracks where you can compete in races over rough terrain, although there has been damage caused to the countryside by mountain bikes. Some people cycle to school or work rather than go by car and towns sometimes have special lanes or cycle paths to make cycling safer. It is the Trust's policy to encourage cycling and several cycling paths have been made through properties. (See pages 30/31.) But cycling now is different to the early days when there were hardly any cars on the road, and you must take care.

- Never play on bikes when you are on the road – it could cause an accident.
- Take a cycling training course (details from you local council) and always follow the Highway Code.
- Always wear a proper cycle helmet.
- Make sure drivers can see you by wearing something bright, or fluorescent, during the day and something reflective at night.
- Look after your bike and check it regularly to make sure it is safe to ride.
- Try to choose routes that avoid major roads, roundabouts and difficult right turns.
- Be constantly alert and aware of what other people on the road (especially drivers) are doing.

The bicycles at ERDIGG, Clwyd, include Philip II's boneshaker and several earlier penny farthings, most of which were acquired by Philip Yorke III. The first of his collection was bought for a shilling (about 5p) from a scrap yard in Aberystwyth!

There is a whole room full of bicycles at SNOWSHILL MANOR in Gloucestershire. In the 'Room of 100 wheels', there are 12 boneshakers, a hobby-horse and a penny farthing, not to mention a bath chair, a collection of children's prams, models of a stage coach, a ship and a steam fire engine, and other objects with transport connections,

Charles Wade, who owned Snowshill, gave each room in the house a name and divided his unusual collection carefully among them. His house became so full he moved out to live in a house in the garden!

Superbike!

Bikes have looked very much the same for the past 100 years until the latest technology gave us the LotusSport, a special kind of racing bike. The LotusSport bike is particularly special because of its aerodynamic design which means it moves easily through the air.

It was ridden to victory at the 1992 Olympics in Barcelona by Chris Boardman. He won the gold medal, lapping his opponent, in the 4,000 metres individual pursuit. It was the first British cycling gold medal for 70 years.

Here is a picture of a bike. Can you put the labels in the right places?

mudguard	chain	crank
pedal	handlebars	brake
tyre rim	spoke	gears

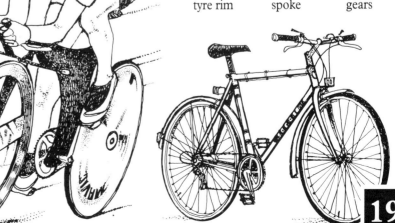

19

Horseless carriages

The shape of things to come

Who could have imagined, when the first petrol-driven car was built in 1885, how important the motor car would become in everyday life? The private car has revolutionised road transport in this century, enabling us to travel where we want and when we want.

However, the first self-propelled road vehicle bore no resemblance to the streamlined and comfortable cars we know today. Nicholas Cugnot's steam wagon, built in France in 1769, had three wooden cartwheels, a huge boiler and a bench to sit on. It was heavy, very slow, and difficult to control.

In the early 1800s, two British engineers, Richard Trevithick and Sir Goldsworthy Gurney, built steam road-carriages, but in Britain, further inventions were held back by a new law.

Slow motion

The Locomotive and Highways Act of 1865 was instigated by the wealthy stage-coach owners and railway companies who wanted to prevent competition. The Act imposed a speed limit of 4 mph (6½ km/h) on country roads and even less in towns. A man on foot waving a red flag had to walk in front of all self-propelled vehicles! When the law was eventually abolished, in 1896, a special rally from London to Brighton was held to celebrate. This is now a famous annual event for veteran cars.

We have the technology!

The first major technological breakthrough came in 1860 when a Belgian, Jean-Joseph Etienne Lenoir (1822-1900) designed the internal combustion engine, using gas as a fuel. Until then engines had always been steam-powered. Lenoir's engine was smaller, lighter and more economical than others, making it ideally suited to road vehicles. In 1877, a German, Nikolaus Otto went one step further by adapting it to run on petrol.

Between 1885 and 1886, two Germans, Karl Benz and Gottlieb Daimler produced the first petrol-driven vehicles. The Benz car was a three-wheeler and carried two people. Its nickname was the 'automobile' or 'horseless carriage'. The Daimler had four wheels. The two men were great rivals until their two companies merged in 1926 to create Mercedes-Benz.

Rudolf Diesel, also German, invented yet another kind of engine which burns heavy oil, now known as diesel, instead of the more refined and expensive petrol. Diesel did not realise it at the time, but this engine was later to prove ideal for heavy vehicles such as buses, trucks and trains.

Activity:
Which came first? Can you put the following vehicles in chronological order?

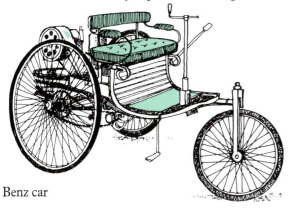

Benz car

Morris Minor

Mini

Ford Model T

and label a b c d   Order: - - - -

Enough to drive you crazy!

Early motoring cannot have been much fun. The first cars had no windscreens, roof or windows! Passengers wore heavy coats and wrapped rugs around their legs to keep warm! Drivers often wore goggles to keep the dust out of their eyes. Women wore veils. Cars were unreliable and because there were still not many garages, drivers had to be mechanics as well! The whole tyre had to be taken off to mend a puncture and cars soon started carrying a spare wheel for emergencies. Until 1919, when the first petrol filling station opened, petrol had to be bought from chemists!

Driving required a lot of skill – the brakes were not very good and steering was difficult. In towns, there were trams and trolley buses to avoid, not to mention horses and carts, people riding bikes and pedestrians who were not yet used to the speed of these new vehicles.

Cars were, not surprisingly, unpopular with a lot of people. They were noisy and dangerous, they churned up dust from the roads and polluted the air with exhaust fumes. Sir Vauncey Harpur Crewe, who owned Calke Abbey in Derbyshire from 1886 to 1924, banned motor vehicles on his estate. Anyone visiting the house had to leave their car at the main gate and be collected by horse and carriage. Ironically his son, Richard Harpur Crewe, was very keen on cars. There is a photo of him in the house at the wheel of his own car.

Once cars began to sell, designs improved and speeds increased. Hoods and upholstery provided greater comfort and pneumatic tyres gave a smoother ride on the new tarmacadam road surfaces. By the 1920s most road transport, including lorries and buses, was motorised.

Big business

Affordable Fords

Early cars were handmade to order and expensive – until an American called Henry Ford (1863-1947) decided to make a simple car that would appeal to everyone and produce the largest possible number at the lowest possible cost. At first, they were built one at a time – one car was finished before the next one was started. Later cars were put together on stands or benches that could be moved along from one team of workers to the next. Each team did just one job. To speed up the process even further, Ford introduced a moving assembly line – the bare chassis was put on at one end and emerged complete at the other, ready to be driven off. The first mass produced car, on sale in 1909, was the Model T or 'Tin Lizzie'.

In 1911 Ford set up a factory at Trafford Park in Manchester. British companies were forced to compete and Morris was first to introduce similar methods to his Cowley factory in Oxford, soon followed by Austin at Longbridge in Birmingham.

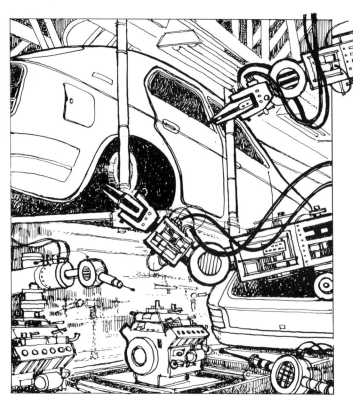

Boom time

Many people's first experience of motor vehicles was as drivers and mechanics during the First World War. This helped influence attitudes afterwards. By 1930 driving licences in Britain reached one million for the first time and two million by 1939. New controls became essential and between 1930 and 1934 new traffic acts introduced traffic lights, pedestrian crossings and a 30mph speed limit in built-up areas, as well as compulsory driving tests, car insurance and penalties for careless driving.

The real car boom began in the 1950s when more and more people could afford to buy a car. The first British motor way – the M1 – was opened in 1958. In 1959 Austin launched the Mini and the British car manufacturing industry was at its peak. Soon it was to be overtaken by its competitors; France, Italy, Germany and especially Japan, who now lead the world in the production of low-price family cars. In order to compete, the motor industry has pioneered the use of high technology in design and engineering. Some cars are now built by robots!

Famous names

In 1905, in Britian, Charles Rolls teamed up with Henry Royce to build superior quality motor cars. Today, everyone has heard of the Rolls Royce.

Ferdinand Porsche, a German, started his career with Daimler, then in 1934 he designed the Beetle for the Volkswagen company. The Beetle had its engine in the back not under the bonnet like other cars. It was made in factories all over the world for more than 40 years. Later, with his son, he designed the first Porsche sports car, now among the world's top-selling luxury cars.

Another world-wide success was the British Mini, designed by Alec Arnold Issigonis, who was also responsible for the Morris Minor. The Mini was launched in 1959 and is still made today.

Rudyard Kipling, the famous author of *The Jungle Book* and the *Just So Stories*, lived at Bateman's, East Sussex, between 1902 and 1936. Kipling loved driving. He and his wife often went on motoring holidays and he kept diaries of his motor tours. His vintage 1928 Rolls-Royce still stands in the garage for visitors to admire.

There is a 1907 Rover at Erdigg, Clwyd. It was bought in the 1920s from the chimney sweep, who bought it from the Rector of Marchwiel! There are also two Austins (1924 and 1927 models) there.

Lord Hesketh, related to the Heskeths of Rufford Old Hall in Cheshire, used to race motorbikes in his youth, before moving on to Formula 1 racing cars

Did you know that...

In 1964, Malcolm Campbell made history when he drove his specially designed car, 'Bluebird', at the record speed of 301 mph. The current land speed record was set by Richard Noble in 1983. In his machine, 'Thrust 2', he reached a speed of 633 mph!

Transport takes off!

Up, up and away!

People have always wanted to fly. Even in Ancient Greece there was a legend which told of Icarus, who flew too near the sun wearing wings made of wax and feathers. The wax melted and Icarus fell into the sea. Leonardo da Vinci (1452 -1519) was probably the first person to create aeroplanes and even helicopters, although only on paper. No-one actually made a realistic attempt to fly until about 300 years later.

In 1783, the first passenger carrying balloon was designed by the Montgolfier brothers, Etienne and Joseph. The passengers on its maiden voyage were a sheep, a cockerel and a duck! They travelled half a mile over Paris in eight minutes.

Those magnificent men...

The first person to fly a plane with an engine was an American, Orville Wright. On 17 December 1903, he flew 36 metres on his first flight! Orville and his brother, Wilbur, made three more flights on that historic day. The farthest they flew was 260 metres. It is hard to believe that only 16 years later two British aviators would be flying across the Atlantic.

In 1919, John Alcock and Arthur Brown flew from Newfoundland to Ireland in a Vickers Vimy bomber. During their epic flight of 16 hours and 27 minutes, Brown had to clamber out on to the wings to chip off ice!

Charles Lindbergh was the first person to fly solo across the Atlantic. His plane was called 'Spirit of St Louis'.

...and women

In 1930, Britain's Amy Johnson flew on her own from London to Australia in her Gipsy Moth aeroplane, 'Jason', stopping only to refuel. A sandstorm forced her to make an emergency landing in the desert near Baghdad, but she achieved her goal, reaching Australia after 19 days of flying. During World War II(1939-1945) she became a delivery pilot, flying new planes from factories to airfields.

Amelia Earhart became the first woman to fly solo across the Atlantic in 1928. In 1935 she made an even longer solo flight across the Pacific. Two years later, attempting to fly around the world, she disappeared and no-one knows what happened to her.

Jean Batten, from New Zealand, completed the first solo flight between England and New Zealand in 1936. Jacqueline Cochran was the first woman to fly faster than the speed of sound.

Battle in the skies

The aeroplane made an enormous impact on warfare. It was quickly developed into a fighting and bombing machine and the Royal Air Force was soon as important as the army and the navy. The Spitfire and Hurricane are famous for their part in the Battle of Britain during the summer of 1940, when the German air force – the Luftwaffe – made repeated air attacks on Britain. On 15 September, hundreds of German aircraft attacked London docks and the Southampton area, resulting in an air battle over the whole of south England which lasted all day. The German High Command finally had to admit that they could not destroy Britain's air defences.

War aces

One of the most famous First World War pilots was the German Baron von Richtofen – the Red Baron – who flew a red Fokker triplane. He became the top war ace, shooting down 80 enemy aircraft.

The avenue of elm trees at Wimploe Hall in Cambridgeshire was used as a landmark for bomber pilots in World War II. The elms were destroyed by Dutch Elm disease in the 1970s but the avenue was replanted with lime trees because of its importance in the war.

T E Lawrence – better known as 'Lawrence of Arabia' – became a hero in the First World War when he helped the Arabs fight the Turks. He later joined the RAF. In 1935, when Lawrence was discharged from the Air Force and had returned to live at Clouds Hill in Dorset, he was tragically killed in a motorbike accident.

Orford Ness, off the Suffolk coast, was formerly owned by the Ministry of Defence. Barnes Wallis tested his famous 'bouncing bomb' there and Robert Watson-Watt carried out early experiments with radar. It has been the site of defence research since 1915.

Round the world in 9 days…

In 1986, Dick Rutan and Jeanna Yeager of the USA made the first non-stop flight around the world in their plane, 'Voyager', which was designed so that it could hold more than three times its own weight in fuel. It took them 9 days.

Jet set

Frank Whittle was an officer in the RAF when he had the idea for the jet engine. He worked on his idea for years in his spare time until the government gave him money to develop it during World War II.

The first passenger-carrying jet aircraft entered service with the British Overseas Airways Corporation in 1952. The 'de Havilland Comet' flew twice as fast as any existing propeller-driven airliner. The number of people travelling by air grew so dramatically that the Boeing company built their 747 'Jumbo' jet, which carries up to 500 passengers and cruises at a speed of more than 600 mph (900km/hr).

In 1976, air travel went supersonic. Concorde, which flies faster than the speed of sound, was built jointly by Britain and France and is the only Western commercial supersonic airliner.

Quiz

Match the airline name to the country and draw in the correct national flag designs

Airline	Country	Flag
Lufthansa	Australia	
Aeroflot	Spain	
Virgin	America	
Pan Am	Britain	
Quantas	Germany	
Iberia	Russia	

25

Tickets to ride

Between the lines

In the early 1800s, most people walked to work, but as towns began to spread the need for better public transport grew. The first horse-drawn tram was on Southend Pier, in Essex, in 1846, but the system quickly spread to large towns throughout Britain and encouraged more and more people to live away from town centres. Early trams ran on raised tracks, like a railway, making it easier for the horses to pull. This was dangerous in busy streets, so they were later sunk into the road, level with the surface, to form the more familiar tramlines.

During the late nineteenth century, some trams ran on steam power, but most were fitted with the newly invented electric motor, taking their power from overhead cables. Electric trams were cheaper, cleaner and faster. The first appeared along the sea front at Brighton in August 1883, shortly followed by the Giant's Causeway electric tramway in Northern Ireland.

September 1885 saw the opening of one of the most famous electric tramway systems in the world – Blackpool. Holidaymakers can still enjoy a ride on trams there today and during the famous 'Illuminations' they are brightly decorated with coloured lights.

Trams now look set for a revival. They are a cleaner, more 'environmentally friendly' alternative to cars in city centres. Some cities, such as Manchester, have decided to solve their transport problems by reintroducing a modern version.

Off the rails

The first trolleybus ran in Britain in 1911. Like trams, they collected power from overhead wires but they didn't run on rails. Tramlines caused many accidents. Trolleybuses were also safer because they could pull in to the side of the road to let people get on and off, instead of having to stop in the middle. By 1939 more than half the trams had been replaced by trolleybuses until they in turn were replaced by diesel buses.

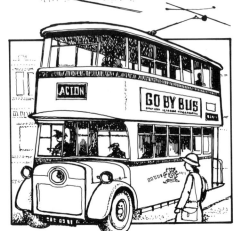

Going underground

London had the world's first underground railway. The Metropolitan Line was the first to open in 1863. Other systems, such as the one in Paris, were to take the shortened name of 'Metro', although in London it has always been known as the 'tube'. Originally, it had open coaches and steam locomotives.

To avoid demolishing buildings, the railway was built mainly underneath existing roads. Tunnels were built by a process called 'cut-and-cover'. A wide trench was dug along the street for the tracks and stations then covered in again. Deeper lines were later built by sinking shafts into the ground and then burrowing through the earth with a large circular iron 'shield'.

Modern underground trains are very different from early ones. The Victoria Line has trains which are operated automatically by electric signals picked up from the rails. They drive and stop themselves!

On the buses

George Shillibeer introduced the first omnibus, as it was called, in 1829. It was pulled by three horses, side by side, and carried 22 passengers. Later models were drawn by only two horses but a third and even fourth was always kept in reserve for steep hills.

Early motor buses were unreliable. They broke down so often it was impossible to have timetables and there were no such things as bus stops – you had to jump into the middle of the road and wave your arms to be picked up!

A piece of string, running along the ceiling inside the bus, was attached to a large wooden ring on the driver's arm. Anyone who wanted to get off just pulled the string to tell the driver to stop.

As buses became busier, passengers were given a ticket to show that they had paid their fare. Until quite recently, buses had a conductor as well as a driver – someone who took the money. Now most buses have machines which do this job.

Buses transformed people's way of life, especially in the country. They still play an important part in many people's lives – especially the elderly and disabled.

Maze

Follow the bus routes to see which number bus will take you to the country house. Answer on page 32.

Upstairs, downstairs!

The big red double-deckers are a famous tourist attraction in London, but how did they originate? Back in the mid 1800s, people perching on top of single-decker buses were becoming a common sight, so some companies started to place two long seats or benches, back to back, on the roofs of their buses. The way up was via a ladder at the back. They were nicknamed 'knifeboards'.

Many knifeboards had so-called 'decency boards' which not only stopped passengers falling off the roof but also prevented passers-by glimpsing the bare ankles of any ladies who had dared to climb on the top deck!

By 1881, double-deckers had 'garden seats' in pairs either side of a gangway and a proper staircase at the back.

Lorry loads of people

Some buses, called charabancs in the 1920s, were built after the First World War by taking a lorry and fixing rows of seats across it, each row with its own door. A pleasant way of travelling provided the weather was fine, they were popular for excursions and tours.

Several Trust properties in London can be reached by public transport. Here are just a few:

BLEWCOAT SCHOOL, Westminster (tube: St James's Park, District Line)
CARLYLE'S HOUSE, Chelsea (tube: Sloane Square, District Line)
EASTBURY MANOR HOUSE, Barking (tube: Upney, District Line)
FENTON HOUSE, Hampstead (tube: Hampstead, Northern Line)
GEORGE INN, Southwark (tube: London Bridge, Northern Line)
MORDEN HALL PARK, Morden (tube: Morden, Northern Line)
OSTERLEY PARK, Isleworth (tube: Osterley, Piccadilly Line)
SUTTON HOUSE, Hackney (tube: Manor House, Piccadilly Line, Bethnal Green, Central Line)

Safe journey!

Heroic rescue

On the night of 7 September 1838, a paddle steamer – the 'Forfarshire' – was wrecked in a storm off the coast of Northumberland. Everyone on board would have drowned had it not been for the bravery of the lighthouse keeper, William Darling and his young daughter, Grace. Grace became a national heroine and she and her father were awarded medals for their courage.

The drama of that night is captured on a mural in the Central Hall at Wallington, in Northumberland. It is one of eight panels, painted by William Bell Scott, which illustrate epic scenes from Northumbrian history.

Today there are coast guard stations and lifeboats to help ships in trouble. Helicopters are also used for rescue work.

Guiding lights

Lighthouses help to guide ships through dangerous waters.

The Souter Lighthouse, Tyne and Wear, was built in 1871. It was the first reliable lighthouse in the world, containing the most advanced technology of the day. Many later models in other parts of the country were based on it. In more than 100 years of operation, the light has only gone out twice – once through mechanical failure and once when the keeper fell asleep! Today, the lighthouse no longer does its traditional job but it is still kept in full working order.

Rules of the road

Child pedestrians and cyclists between the ages of 10 and 15 are most at risk on the road, having more accidents each year than any other group. One in 15 children will be injured on the roads before their sixteenth birthday.

Are you always careful when you cross the road?

Remember:

Choose a safe place to cross. Always use a zebra or pelican crossing if you can. Some people, such as police men and women, traffic wardens or lollipop people will help you cross the road.

STOP at the pavement behind the kerb.

LOOK both ways for traffic.

LISTEN for cars coming.

When you are sure it is safe, walk across the road, looking and listening all the time.

Wear light-coloured (fluorescent) clothes in the daytime and something reflective at night so that drivers can see you more easily.

Stand under a street lamp while looking and listening when it is dark and walk well away from the kerb – especially in foggy weather.

Safer by design

Laws, such as speed limits and the compulsory wearing of seat belts, have helped to make motoring safer, but one of the biggest advances in safety for car occupants has been the design of cars themselves. New car models are subjected to strict tests with dummy people inside. Standard features in many cars now include safety glass which shatters instead of breaking on impact, head restraints, better tyres and anti-lock braking.

Behind the wheel

Drivers are responsible for many accidents. A major cause of fatal and serious injury accidents is alcohol. Anti-drink-drive campaigns and stricter laws should help to reduce the number of accidents caused by drunken drivers.

Speeding is also a major cause of road accidents. The faster a car is travelling the less choice the driver has of avoiding an accident. Higher speeds also mean more serious (or fatal) accidents. The police have up-to-date technology to help them enforce the law. For example, hand-held radar guns or speed cameras tell them how fast a car is going and if it is breaking the speed limit. Another new idea is a camera set into traffic lights. If a vehicle crosses a junction when the lights are on red, a photo is taken. The date, time and speed are set into the photo frame and the owner of the car is notified that an offence has been committed.

Stop that train!

The signal box plays an important role in safe railway travel. In the early days, trains were prevented from crashing into each other by time intervals. Railway policemen by the side of the track waved coloured flags to signal when a train could move on.

The 'block' system is used on most lines today. Only one train is allowed in one section at a time. A signal warns the driver if there is a train in the section ahead. Then he must stop until the signal shows 'all clear'. Many trains are fitted with automatic warning systems. A buzzer in the cab sounds if a train passes a signal set at 'danger'. Early block system signal men passed messages up and down line by telegraph; now it is computerised.

Many modern trains also have a 'dead man's handle' – a metal lever which the driver holds down to keep the train moving. The moment he lets go, for example if he were to collapse, the train stops.

Did you know that...

Flying is one of the safest ways to travel. An air passenger is more likely to be involved in an accident driving to the airport than flying from it.

Air traffic controllers are responsible for keeping aircraft safely separated from each other. They maintain contact with the aircraft through VHF radio telephone and monitor aircraft movements using radar.

Activity

Here are some road signs. Write the correct label under the sign. Answers on page 32.

_____   _____   _____

_____   _____   _____

Shades of green

The price of progress

In 1904 there were less than 10,000 cars in Britain. Today there are more than 20 million. The motor car may have given people greater freedom and mobility than ever before, but it has also brought us traffic jams, accidents and pollution.

Everyone laughed at Clive Sinclair's electrically driven C5 but we may well need something like it in the future if we continue to use up non-renewable resources such as petrol. Improved technology means that all forms of transport are using less fuel, but the amount of transport, especially road, is still on the increase. One of the biggest problems is congestion. New bypasses may cut through unspoilt countryside but they do reduce the level of traffic in towns. Some town centres are now pedestrianised.

A number of steps have been taken to reduce air pollution and by the year 2,000 most cars on British roads will have catalytic converters and run on unleaded fuel.

Some cities are planning to reintroduce trams to reduce congestion and many have made it safer for cyclists by providing special cycle lanes and tracks.

Troubled waters

The biggest oil spill on record occurred on 24 March 1989 in Southern Alaska, when the oil tanker Exxon Valdez ran aground in Prince William Sound. More than 42 million litres of crude oil spilled out, destroying wildlife and polluting hundreds of kilometres of coastline. Scientists recorded tens of thousands of dead sea otters and birds.

Great efforts have been made to develop effective methods of dealing with oil pollution, such as floating booms and barriers. Chemicals called dispersants help to break up oil, but they can be as harmful to marine life as the oil.

Lessons are learned from each incident, but it seems a great price to pay. The increase in environmental disasters in recent years caused by these huge vessels must call into question the safety of this method of transport for such potentially dangerous cargoes.

Danger! Toads crossing!

When new roads are built special measures are taken to protect wildlife and make sure as little damage as possible is done to the environment. For example, the M40 has 14 badger tunnels and the A12 has a badger bridge! Tunnels for toads and warning signs for drivers are provided at breeding sites where the creatures cross. Grass verges are not mown any more, so that wild flowers can flourish. One verge – on the A1 at Hook Moor in Yorkshire – has been designated a Site of Special Scientific Interest.

Placed in trust

The National Trust with its teams of wardens, foresters, archaeologists and conservation experts is helping to protect the environment in many ways.

The Trust was established in 1895 to preserve permanently land and buildings of historic interest or natural beauty for the benefit of the nation. The Trust does all it can to improve public access to its properties wherever possible. However, many of the Trust's sites attract millions of visitors a year and the facilities they need, such as car parks, can spoil the very landscape the people have come to see. So access to fragile habitats and archaeological sites has to be restricted if they are to be preserved.

Park and ride

A park and ride bus scheme on the Lizard in Cornwall, organised jointly by the Trust and the county council, is helping to reduce the number of cars that clog up country roads.

A series of guided tours introduced people to the idea of parking, catching a bus to the start of a trail and walking back to their cars at their own pace. The trails vary in length and include a Wrecker's Trail and a Naturalist's Trail. It is hoped that this picturesque area might one day be car-free!

Don't miss the bus!

If everyone were to use public transport more there would be less traffic congestion and less pollution:

- Buses and coaches use less energy per passenger than any other form of motorised transport.
- If only 5% of current journeys were made by bus or coach instead of car, a quarter of a million tonnes of pollutants from exhaust emissions would be eliminated annually.
- Double-decker buses carry, on average, as many passengers as 22 cars in around one seventh of the space!

For a list of National Trust properties in London that you can visit by public transport, see page 27.

Off the beaten track

Many disused railways are now important wildlife habitats. At Wallington in Northumberland, the Trust has opened a 7-mile walk making use of two disused railway lines, the Rothbury line (closed in 1963) and the Wannie line (closed in 1966). Way marked paths across the fields link the sections of grassy track.

On your bike!

Cycling is one of the best – and greenest – ways of seeing the countryside. There are paths through many National Trust properties. One of the most popular is the path which begins on the Saltram estate in Devon and runs through the Plymbridge Woods all the way to Dartmoor.

You can also pedal your way round Clumber Park in Nottinghamshire and you don't even need to take your own bike! There are more than 200 bicycles available for people of all ages.

Note to parents/answers

Transport is a popular topic in primary schools which has several links with the National Curriculum. Your child will almost certainly cover it at some stage in Geography, History and Technology.

This book is a compilation of facts and information designed both to entertain and educate. Children will enjoy reading the stories of famous people and events and connecting these to National Trust properties, while gaining a valuable insight into important historical developments.

National Trust properties span a variety of historical periods in a number of ways, and provide an ideal means of exploring different aspects of the development of transport. Children can learn about ways in which people have changed their environment, why different forms of transport are used, and how the transition is made from one means of transport to another. Learning about the history of transport also enables children to learn about everyday lives of men, women and children in the past.

Answers

Page 2:
15 days
How many miles?
Bath   30 miles
York   100 miles
Exeter   18 miles
Chester 62 miles

Page 8:

Who goes there?

Christopher Columbus discovered the Americas for Spain

Vasco da Gama discovered a sea route from Europe to India

Ferdinand Magellan made the first voyage round the world

Sir Francis Drake was the first Englishman to sail round the world

Page 9:

Circumnavigate

Here are 50 words which can be made from the word 'circumnavigate':

gate mate rate crate cage rage game tame name age navigate ate nice mice rice mine vine time vain vane mane cane team tear trim treat eat age ice cure give girt true came tinge cringe ten grave get tag given crime nag gum rum train rain gain rug tug

Page 14/15:
T R A I N

Page 15: Downword

				P
	W			A
	A	S		D
E	S	T		D
U	T	T		I
S	E	P	V	N
T	R	A	I	N
O	L	N	C	G
N	O	C	T	T
	O	R	O	O
		A	R	N
		S	I	
			A	

Page 17:

Trains:
Rocket
Catch Me Who Can
Puffing Billy
Mallard

Boats:
Great Eastern
Mary Rose
Titanic
Golden Hind

Planes:
Voyager
Concorde
Jason
Spirit of St Louis

Page 19: Bike and its labels

Page 21: The correct order is:
a Benz Car   1885
b Ford Model T   1911
c Morris Minor   1948
d Mini   1959

Page 25:

Lufthansa	Germany
Aeroflot	Russia
Virgin	Britain
Pan Am	America
Quantas	Australia
Iberia	Spain

Page 27: Maze - no. 72

Page 29: Road signs

no right turn

no cycling

30 mph speed limit

crossroads

humpback bridge

roadworks

First published in 1994 by National Trust (Enterprises) Ltd, 36 Queen Anne's Gate, London SW1H 9AS

Registered Charity No. 205846

Copyright © The National Trust 1994

All rights reserved. No part of this publication may be reproduced, stored in a retrieval system, or transmitted by any means, electronic, mechanical, photocopying or otherwise, without prior permission of the publisher.

ISBN: 0-7078-0181-8

Designed by Blade Communications, Leamington Spa

Printed by Wing King Tong Ltd., Hong Kong